My Moroccan Village

Written and Illustrated by
Luqman Nagy

Goodwordkidz

This book is dedicated to my second son, 'Abd al-Hay.

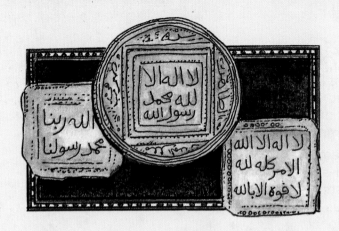

Here are two very old gold and silver coins that belong to my grandfather. The square coin is a silver *dirham* from Cordoba, Al-Andalus (Spain). It was brought to Morocco five hundred years ago when many Muslims were expelled from Spain by the Catholic monarchs King Ferdinand and Queen Isabella. The gold coin is a much older Muwahhid *dinar*. The *kalimah al-shahadah*, beautifully inscribed on each of these coins proclaims Allah's Unity. The inscription on the obverse of the silver coin on the right reads: "There is no deity worthy of worship but Allah. All power belongs to Allah. There is no strength except in Allah." Most cities and towns of northern Morocco have quarters where descendents of Andalusian Muslims reside to this very day.

Goodword Books Pvt. Ltd.
1, Nizamuddin West Market, New Delhi 110 013
Tel. 2435 5454, 2435 6666, 2435 5729 Fax 2435 7333, 2435 7980
e-mail: info@goodwordbooks.com
www.goodwordbooks.com
Printed in India

First published 2003
© Goodword Books, 2003

"Culture" is often defined by anthropologists as a set of shared beliefs, values and behaviours. "Islamic culture", over a period of more than 14 centuries, has been the product of Muslims collectively sharing a common belief in the Unity of Allah and the Prophet-hood of His last messenger, Muhammad ﷺ.

After embracing *din al-haqq al-islam,* peoples as diverse as the Hausa-speaking Fulani of Northern Nigeria and the Uighur Turks of western China have all developed unique cultures that despite obvious differences are unmistakably Islamic in every respect. Traditional Islamic communities still exist today, *Al-Hamdulillah*, and are often referred to as "living museums". For the sincere, well-read and history-conscious Muslim, however, these vestiges of traditional Islamic culture are a legacy to be studied, respected and immensely valued.

One such unique Islamic culture is that of Morocco, a country whose rural and urban Islamic traditions overlap and exhibit to this day a rare example of an Islamic people who have, on the whole, intentionally attempted *not* to "sell out" to the West.

What this book offers our young readers is a passport to a wonderfully rich world in which McDonald's and MTV will never gain entry, *Insha Allah*. 'Abd al-Hay, a bright Moroccan boy of Berber origin, lives in a village in the High Atlas Mountains; through him, the reader will come to understand and appreciate the Islamic culture of his part of *Maghreb al-'Aqsa*, the country that in the 8th century CE became Islam's most westerly outpost.

Morocco is a land of exquisite colour. The illustrations presented here are but one writer's attempt to capture the essence of this culture in colour.

Finally, 'Abd al-Hay welcomes all readers of his world to his world; why not visit him one day?

To you all, my salaams.

King Fahd University
Dhahran, Saudi Arabia

Luqman Nagy
Ramadhan 1422 AH
November 2001

*M*y name is 'Abd al-Hay. I am a twelve year old Moroccan Muslim boy, *Al-Hamdulillah. Tafaddalu fee qaryatuna*, as we say in Moroccan Arabic. "Welcome to our village." My village is called Ait Beni Korchi; it lies just beyond the last hillock.

I live in a beautiful village of many *qasbahs* or large, mud-walled, turreted compounds. So, my area of Morocco in the High Atlas Mountains is called *Belad al-Qusour* or "land of fortified villages". We are Berbers and the design of our buildings (wide at the bottom and narrower at the top) is said to have originated in the skyscraper desert towns of Shibam and Tarim in Southern Arabia (present-day Yemen).

When the Romans first came to North Africa 2,000 years ago, they discovered my ancestors here. We spoke then and still do, a unique language that resembles no other in the world. The Romans, therefore, called us "barbarians" or Berbers. In the Berber language, however, we call ourselves *Imazighen*, or "free men". At home we speak the Shluh Berber dialect. We do not write our mother tongue today, but on large rock faces in the Sahara Desert there are examples of very old Berber language inscriptions using a unique alphabet.

It is late summer, but the beautiful Atlas Mountains still have snow on them. These mountains provide Morocco with much of its water from fast flowing rivers which help us irrigate our fields of wheat and our date groves. We store most of our wheat in spectacular mud tower granaries called *agadirs*.

As you can see, we use red earth as a building material here in the mountains. In some areas, our houses seem to blend right in with the surroundings!

*H*ere is my house in Ait Beni Korchi village. Its walls are constructed of chopped straw and mud: a supreme example of earth architecture. My father and uncle both learned how to build such houses when they were my age. The thick walls help keep our house cool in the long hot summer days and warm during the long cold wintry nights. The colour of our village changes from an orange-rust to a pinkish-red throughout the day. The heavy rains of spring can easily damage our houses, so earth buildings like ours must be repaired each autumn with a mixture of straw and mud.

A lot of cedar, cork and oak trees still grow in the Atlas Mountains. Village carpenters use this wood to design beautiful window frames, some with lattice screening called *mashrabiyyah* that let in cool breezes but flter out sunlight. Very few houses have any glass window panes.

The small white building at the top of the stairs is a *marabout*, the tomb of an extremely pious Muslim who died in our village more than three hundred years ago.

Delicious green and black olives are grown in the lower valleys. We use the oil-press in front of our house to make very tasty olive oil which we collect and store in large earthenware jars.

In late summer, we harvest the large *majdoul* dates which we place in hand-woven baskets. These dates can be kept indefinitely in a cool, dry corner of our house.

The Barbary fig (prickly pear) cactus helps to keep any stray animals away from our vegetable garden. There is no fruit on the cactus plants because of my baby brother; he ate all the fruit yesterday!

$\mathcal{L}$ike everything in my country, Moroccan cooking is unique; it uses wonderful fresh fruits and vegetables in very interesting ways.

The national dish of Morocco, for example, is *couscous* which my mother prepares for us each week after *salat al-juma'*. *Couscous* is steamed semolina wheat kernels cooked with oil, carrots, squash and sometimes big sweet quinces, all topped with stewed mutton or chicken.

Once the *couscous* is ready to eat, my mother places it and all the toppings in a large blue and white hand-painted ceramic bowl. Every family owns at least one such bowl that is used for serving specially prepared meals.

Another delicious Moroccan dish is *tajin*, a stew of meat and vegetables slowly cooked in earthenware pots with conical lids. Would you like to have lunch with us today? *Insha Allah*, you will like my mother's chicken *tajin* which she has cooked with apricots and almonds. My mother always makes *dhikr* when she works in the kitchen. *Masha Allah* I think her chicken *tajin* is the best in all of the Atlas Mountains!

During the long summer, when I am not busy with my studies at school, I look after our vegetable garden. I water and weed the plants daily. This morning I picked some fresh mint for our tea and some delicious ripe tomatoes. Did you know that the tomato was brought from South America to Spain by the Spaniards? It was then brought to Morocco from Al-Andalus by Muslim refugees fleeing from the Inquisition.

We can wash our hands now. Lunch is ready!

$\mathcal{M}$y family and all other inhabitants of Ait Beni Korchi are no longer nomads. We now live in a settled village but still keep many of our old nomadic traditions alive.

Many Berber tribes, however, continue to travel twice yearly with their flocks of sheep and goats from the mild winter lowlands to the much cooler higher summer pastures. My mother, aunts and most women in Ait Beni Korchi practice to some degree the very, very old craft of weaving. This is truly an art perfected by nomads. The weaving of carpets, blankets, capes, tent bands, grain and market bags and other utility items have always had a very practical purpose for the nomad: they are all used by nomads in their daily lives whether on the move or in camp.

In the summer months, we can see Berber tribes camped at the foothills of the High Atlas Mountains, just outside our village. Their black goat hair tents dot the landscape. These Berbers all speak our dialect: Shluh. Each spring when these tribes begin their migration to the mountains, my mother and her sisters all want to buy wool from them. The best quality wool comes from sheep that are first washed in mountain streams and are shorn of their wool only once a year. My mother also gets some wonderful natural dyes to colour the wool. For example, a certain type of dried fig and pomegranate blended together produce a high quality black dye; almond leaves give a beautiful natural yellow.

The Berber villagers of the Atlas also weave a lot of spectacular carpets that can be found for sale in the weekly *souq* or market. My father and I, for example, bought the two carpets here in the *souq al-sebt* (Saturday market); they were both woven by the Ait Ouaouzguite tribe who live to the west of us. They cover the floor of our sitting room where guests are welcomed. Because Islam forbids the representation of animal or human form, all these carpets have wonderful, colourful geometric designs on them. I respect the art of carpet weaving because I know how difficult it is to make a carpet.

Weaving is yet another artistic expression of my country's rich Islamic cultural heritage.

*M*orocco is a very ancient land. Areas that were once sea beds are now high up in the Atlas Mountains. Ever since I was a small child, I have been collecting semi-precious stones like amethyst and many attractive fossils. I never knew what a fossil was until I started school but I collected them just the same because of their interesting designs and shapes.

Fossils like the ones here are commonly found all over the Atlas Mountains in exposed sedimentary rock deposits. When we find them, we carry them home; larger fossils are often cut out of the rock by older boys who use simple cutting tools like picks and chisels.

My teacher at school told us last year that the fossils in my collection are more than 300 million years old and date from a time when our mountain village was deep below the sea! Can we really believe this? The Holy Qur'an doesn't tell us precisely when Allah created the Earth, but as a Muslim, knowing the exact age of the Earth is not all that important. In *Surah Luqman* (XXXI, 10-11), Allah reminds us that "He set on the Earth mountains standing firm... such is the Creation of Allah". What *is* important is to credit the Creator for His masterful Creation.

These are three beautiful ammonites and one trilobite from my fossil collection. Ammonites were mollusks (a type of shellfish) that lived along with trilobites arthropods like crabs in the prehistoric seas. The examples here are all "mold" fossils which were formed when the ammonites and trilobites died on the sea floor. All soft parts of the animal decomposed. Then, the skeletons or other harder body parts eventually turned to rock when sediments pressed down on them.

All of my friends have fossil collections. They often sell their specimens to foreign tourists who drive past on the main highway through the mountains. I think I'm a "professional" fossil collector: I never sell any of my finds!

Fossils to me are but curious reminders of a very distant past of which we know little. Indeed, in the end, Allah is the All-Knowing, the Most Wise.

ناجي

$\mathscr{M}$y father is a *mu'allim*, a skilled potter and ceramic tile maker. He takes local red clay from nearby cliffs, adds water and mixes the moist clay with his feet. He learned his craft from other master tile makers in Ait Beni Korchi.

Making *zillij* or mosaic cut-tiles is a complex process. Designs are first drawn on large sheets of paper. The patterns are individually coloured, numbered and then cut. The cut-out patterns are placed on tiles of the same colour. Hammers, chisels and files are used to cut the tiles and smooth the edges. Finally, these precisely cut pieces of *zillij* are placed on a soft plaster surface to form the design that you can see here.

The kilns, or "ovens", my father uses to fire his tiles lie just outside of our village ; they are centuries old and have always been in use. When the tiles are ready, my father takes them to the first kiln used for firing the "raw" ceramic material. The second kiln seals or "fixes" the colours. He uses willow wood (stripped of its bark) or ground up olive pits as a fuel to fire the kiln. Just as carpet weavers use plants to make their dyes, ceramic tile makers make their own beautiful "natural" glazes. To produce the clear blue colour, my father mixes lead, sand and a special stone found only near Rabat, the capital city of Morocco. For yellow, he mixes lead, sand, rust and a stone found only in the area around Fez.

My father is not only a master of cut-tile mosaic, but can also produce work such as the Arabic calligraphy you can see above the *zillij*. This involves a difficult process. First, a large slab of reddish-gray clay covered with a deep purple/black glaze is fired. After firing, the Arabic inscription is drawn onto the glazed tile. Finally, the tile is chiseled away revealing only the Arabic writing in relief.

Once again, a connection can be made between my country, Morocco and Al-Andalus (Spain). Muslim immigrants who were fleeing the persecution in the 13th century, brought their ceramic tile making expertise with them to Morocco. The tradition is alive and well in our part of the Islamic world, *Al-Hamdulillah*, Many mosaic tile designs like this one resemble *zillij* found today in old buildings in Cordoba and Granada in Spain.

Finally, the Moroccan Arabic word for ceramic tile: *zillij* (plural *zulayj*) has passed into the Spanish and Portuguese languages where the word *azulejo* refers to the blue and white ceramic tiles produced in the Hispano-Arabic style.

Al-Hamdulillah, today I am visiting the *souq al-khamis* (Thursday market). *Souqs* (markets) are named after the days of the week. For example, *souq al-ahad* is the "Sunday" market. *Al-Hamdulillah*, market days are very interesting and exciting, especially for children. They also offer an opportunity for friends to meet and catch up on the latest news.

After *salat al-fajr*, most men and boys in the village prepare their donkeys or horses for the long ride to the market. Today, I will help my father to try to sell two large baskets of *majdoul* dates which he has loaded onto either side of our donkey.

Tomorrow is *juma'* and I want to buy a new *taqiyyah* (prayer cap) and a pair of yellow *babouche* (soft leather slippers) to wear to the mosque. Look at the beautiful selection of *taqiyyahs* for sale on that eucalyptus tree! In Morocco, these beautifully crafted prayer caps are knitted only by men. The yellow leather *babouches* are also made by men. Moroccan leather is of an excellent quality. Inside our homes and outside, we all wear heel-less slippers. The yellow kind is the most popular and many are sold on market day.

Al-Hamdulillah, everything is for sale in the market today! Can you see my father's *majdoul* dates and my aunt's Berber carpet? The large earthenware pots are hand-made *gidrahs*, traditionally made for cooking *couscous*. Local spices and herbal medicines are also sold. The green powder you can see is *henna'* which when mixed with water is used to paint semi-permanent designs on women's hands, palms and feet. It also dyes the hair a reddish colour. Berber villagers sell fresh eggs, chickens, fresh vegetables and all kinds of cereals and seeds. The market is full of wonderful sights and sounds!

With the hundreds of pack animals that arrive on market day, blacksmiths are always very busy fitting horseshoes. For some villagers this is the only opportunity to buy "new shoes" for their animals!

The pine forests of the High Atlas Mountains produce a superb honey that we use as a medicine. My friend Nuh weaves beehive baskets. Today he is very happy because he has sold many. My father is also very pleased. He has sold all his dates so I now have a beautiful new *taqiyyah* and a new pair of *babouche*, *Al-Hamdulillah*.

16

Al-Hamdulillah, it is the Holy Month of Ramadhan! *Ramadan Karim*, as we say in Arabic! All Muslims have waited eleven long months to welcome the most special of months. As Allah says in the Holy Qur'an: "The month of Ramadhan in which the Qur'an was revealed".

Ramadhan this year is in winter. Each day at sunset we walk at a brisk pace to our mosque where we meet for breaking the fast. As the *muezzin* calls Muslims to prayer, we break our fast with dates and *zam zam* water which my uncle brought all the way from Holy Makkah last *hajj*. After *al-maghreb* prayer, we walk home and enjoy a light '*iftar* of hard-boiled eggs with cumin seed powder, freshly-squeezed orange juice and lots of hot whole wheat flat bread eaten with hearty *harirah* soup made of chick peas, lentils, celery, tomatoes and meat broth.

Taraweeh prayers are recited after every *salat al-'eisha* during Ramadhan. During the last ten days, however, the *muezzin* places a large brass lantern atop the minaret. The light, visible to all in the valley, is a reminder of the importance of this blessed month - the importance of these last days of Ramadhan when we are all seeking the bounteous blessings of *lailat al-qadr*, the night which the Qur'an says is "better than a thousand months".

Al-Hamdulillah, in the evening our mosque fills with worshippers who stay until morning prayers; our mosque rings with the beautiful recitation of Allah's Word. We have a very beautiful *tajweed* (style of recitation) that is unique to Morocco. As children we learn this when we study and memorize the Qur'an. Fathers, uncles, cousins and nephews, grandfathers and grandsons all sit in *halaqaat* or "circles" and recite Allah's Book and then pray. May Allah the Almighty accept our intention, our fasting, our good deeds, and all our '*ibadah* and *dua*'s!

This Ramadhan, a stork's nest adorns our minaret. Storks migrate from Europe each year to winter with us in Morocco. The *muezzin* says there are two eggs in the nest. *Insha Allah*, they will hatch before or during "*Eid al-Fitr*!"

I have studied the Holy Qur'an with other village children here in our mosque. Mosques in Morocco are quite plain on the inside. Walls are white-washed and the floor and columns are covered with beautifully hand-woven reed matting. Woolen carpets are rarely used in traditional Moroccan mosques. Special *ustadhs*, or master weavers, produce these mats in villages in the lowlands where the reeds grow. Do you see the unique Arabic inscription painted on the wall? This is a very famous example of Maghrebi calligraphy written by the *khattat* al-Qandusi more than 150 years ago. A village calligrapher copied the words "Allah" and "Muhammad" in black paint.

I love our mosque. It is *bait AIlah* as well as being *bait al-hikmah*, a "House of Wisdom". We study Islamic sciences: *tafseer, fiqh, hadeeth, seerah* and *mantiq* in the traditional way. Our teacher sits on the wooden *kursi* which faces the *qiblah* wall. This *kursi* is hundreds of years old, as old as the mosque's *minbar*.

Today we studied the *seerah* of 'Ibn Ishaq. It is wonderful to read about the life of our beloved Prophet Muhammad ﷺ. By the way, several important members of the Prophet's family came to Morocco in the very early days of Islam. Even our present king's (Muhammed VI) family, the *'Alawiyyah*, are direct descendents of Hadhrat 'Ali (*radhi Allahu 'anhu*). Morocco is, therefore, officially known as the "Sherifian Kingdom of the Maghreb".

On the back wall of the mosque we hang the wooden writing boards we use as small children to practice and learn Arabic writing. My first board is still there; it is now used by my three year old brother "Abd al-Khalaq.

After praying *salah* in this mosque, I often think about our rich and glorious Islamic history. Above my head is a huge bronze lamp. Our *imam* told me that this was made from a bell that had been taken from a church in Al-Andalus hundreds of years ago by the Muwahhid Berbers when they were waging war with the Christians in Spain.

For years my teacher has reminded us of the importance of the Qur'anic command: *Iqra'* ("Read!"). I am studying very hard to memorize the entire Qur'an, *Al-Hamdulillah*. When I am older, I would like to go to study Islam, *din al-haqq*, at the 1,000 year old *jamiyah al-qarawiyyin* in the royal city of Fez, the religious "heart" of my country. With Allah's help, I would like to be a successful teacher who teaches others to "read".

20

*H*ere is my old *saboorah* that my younger brother 'Abd al-Khalaq now uses for copying *surahs*. We never use notebooks or pencils. Wooden boards like this are the traditional method that is still used by Muslim children all over North Africa: Morocco, Algeria, the *Sahel* countries, and as far south as Senegal and Northern Nigeria.

Islam came to Morocco in the first century *hegira*. Shortly thereafter, Tariq 'ibn Ziyad, the famous Berber commander, led the first group of Muslims across into Al-Andalus (Spain) almost 1,300 years ago. Our history, both ancient and modern, has always been closely linked with that of Al-Andalus. Muslim families in many small towns and cities of northern Morocco still trace their origins back to Al-Andalus. Many of these families own precious hand-written copies of the Holy Qur'an that were brought with them from Al-Andalus hundreds of years ago. Such Qur'ans were written in the Andalusian script which resembles the *Maghrebi* script still taught in Morocco today. My teacher told me that in the past, Moroccan scribes (copiers of the Qur'an) were taught the *Maghrebi* script by writing complete words, not single letters.

We learn to read and write the *khat al-maghrebi* even before we begin regular school. We write with hand-cut reed pens which are dipped into a water-based black ink. After my teacher has corrected my writing, he washes my board clean with water. Two Arabic letters in the *Maghrebi* script are written differently from standard writing practice: standard /f/ *fa* becomes a *fa* with the dot written below the letter while the standard /q/ *qaf* is written with a single dot above (resembling the standard /f/)!

My little brother has written three verses (117-119) from *surat al-nisa'*. See how he has written the letter *qaf* in the word *qaala* and the letter *fa* in the word *mafroodha*.

Al-Hamdulillah, I love learning and seeing others learn. Yesterday, our teacher was very busy with other children. He told me to teach *surah al-qari'ah* to my baby brother and his little friends. What a reward when "my pupils" learned to read, write and memorize this blessed *surah*! For the first time in my life, I actually felt like a teacher. May Allah always increase my knowledge to enable me to become the best possible Muslim and the best possible teacher - one who can really make a difference. *Ameen*.

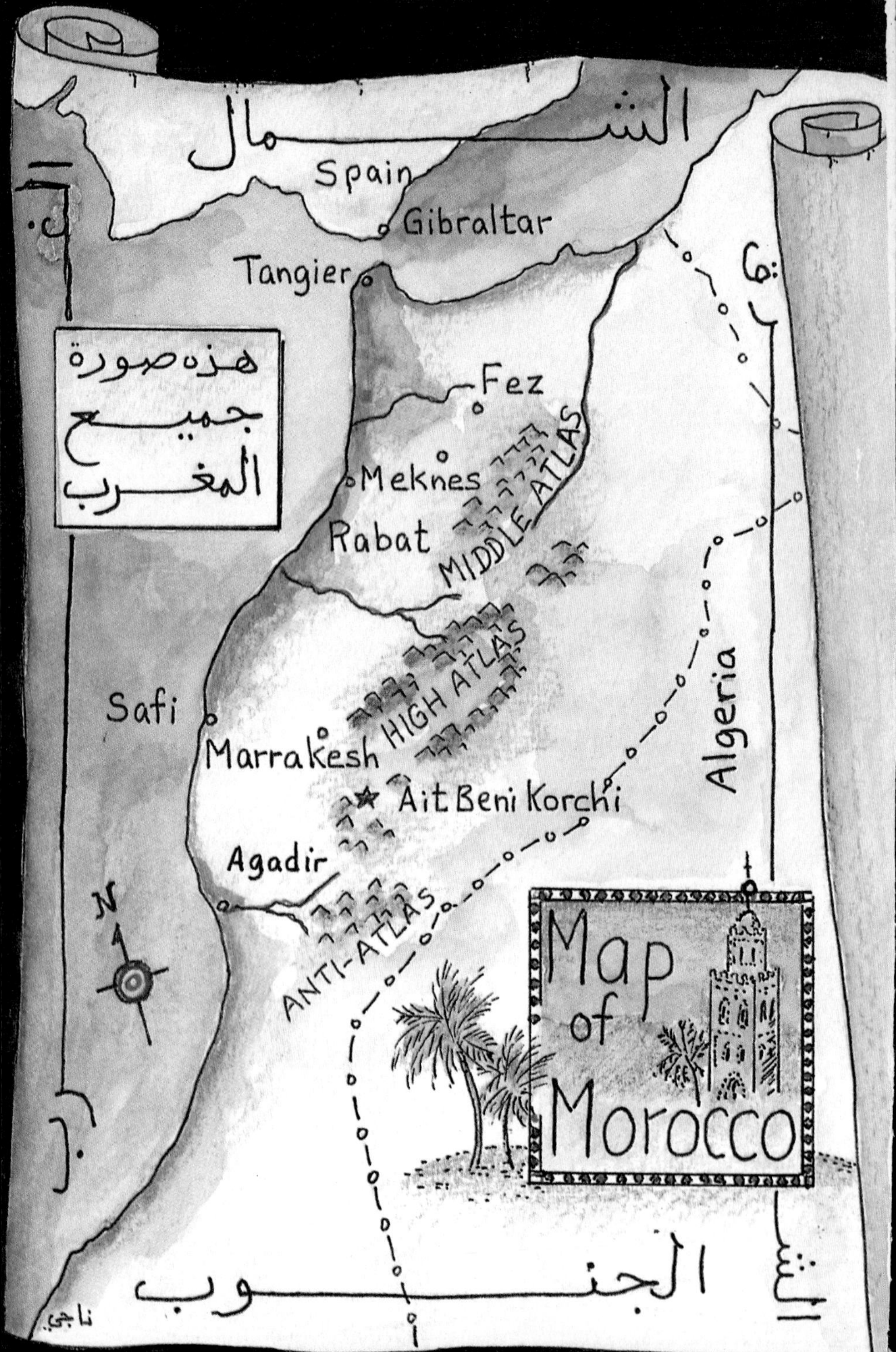
الشمال
Spain
Gibraltar
Tangier
هذه صورة
جميع
المغرب
Fez
Meknes
Rabat
MIDDLE ATLAS
HIGH ATLAS
Safi
Marrakesh
Ait Beni Korchi
Agadir
ANTI-ATLAS
Algeria
N
Map of Morocco
الجنوب
ناجي